THE Little Book OF Theatre Games

A Lillenas® DRAMA RESOURCE

THE Little Book OF Theatre Games

Interactive Material from Custer & Hoose Workshops

BY JIM CUSTER & BOB HOOSE

WITH GARY LEE REED

Lillenas® PUBLISHING COMPANY
KANSAS CITY, MO 64141

Printed in the United States

Lillenas Publishing Company
Drama Permission Office
P.O. Box 419527
Kansas City, MO 64141
Phone: 816-931-1900 • fax: 816-753-4071
E-mail: drama@lillenas.com

Contents

The Little Book of Theatre Games Introduction

This book of exercises is designed to give the drama enthusiast some useful tools for rehearsals, for classroom and workshop activities, or for simple warm-ups. Theatre games help teach acting principles such as creativity, character development, social community, focus, imagination, physical awareness, and self-esteem.

IT'S NEXT MONTH ALREADY

About 14 years ago, I started using and soon became an advocate of theatre games. My friend Paul McCusker and I started a small drama ministry in Thousand Oaks, California, and we decided to incorporate a few games we had picked up from an acting class. What soon became evident was how effective these exercises could be in teaching both the actors and us budding directors how to do our jobs. Not long after that, I had the good fortune of teaming up with Jim Custer in what was soon to become Custer and Hoose. We used theatre games in our performance preparation and began teaching them in our drama seminars. Along the way, people consistently asked, "Where do we get more of these games?" We dutifully pointed these wise adventurers to various secular sources, all the while lamenting the fact that some Christian publisher didn't add a games book or two to their catalog. "Why don't you guys write one?" came the impassioned retort. Why not indeed. However, as much as we loved the use of the games, we weren't confident that we could actually create a book of them. That's when we turned to Gary Reed. We knew Gary from past touring years together with the comedy drama group Jeremiah People. Since 1982, however, Gary has immersed himself in many aspects of professional theatre in Los Angeles. He has performed in a wide variety of stage and film roles, dabbled in commercial work, become technical director for several theatres, and won an honorary Emmy for his art direction. This guy is too much. What was most important to us, however, was his work with an improvisational theatre troupe. Gary was a regular treasure chest of games. That's when we all began our quest to get this book together. People asked, "When will it be done?" We'd say, "We hope next month." We said that so often that it became a joke, though I must admit we weren't laughing all the time. Well, after three years of effort, it's finally next month.

OVERCOME FEAR AND COMPLACENCY

You might be asking, "What's all the fuss? I've played silly games before, but what I need to do is to get on with the real work of my local drama ministry. I need to teach my actors how to act."

That is precisely what theatre games are all about. Theatre games are essentially nonthreatening exercises that help teach acting principles. They can graduate from very simple to very complicated, and they challenge us to leap over the stumbling blocks that hinder us as actors. One of the stumbling blocks we encounter is fear—fear of failure, fear of forgetting our lines, fear of looking stupid in front of our peers, fear of looking fat in this shirt, and the list goes on. Another is complacency. We get so comfortable with a role or an approach to acting that we can no longer stretch beyond those boundaries. It's less threatening to do what we've always done and never face the uncomfortable terror of change. Playing games helps us leap over these hurdles by allowing us to have fun. While we're all enjoying ourselves, we forget about the things that are scary or a little too difficult; and in the midst of play, we learn how to reach our goals.

THE GAMES

The games themselves have been around for years—adapted or handed down in workshops and classes, wearing differing names and labels. One of the original sources of theatre games is Viola Spolin. It was in Ms. Spolin's groundbreaking theatre workshops that most of the exercises and theatre sports activities used today were given birth.

You'll notice we've listed the theatre games in this book within five categories: Team Building, Body and Movement, Spontaneity, Give and Take, and Character Development. We've even included a bonus section of vocal warm-ups. We believe these choices represent some of the basic building blocks of good acting and a healthy drama ministry.

We've also listed the exercises by increasing level of difficulty within each category. Starting easy and working up to a greater challenge is always the best way to go. As you get to know them, you will discover that many of the games actually overlap and can fit into several of the listed categories. In some cases, we've tried to draw your attention to how one game in the book might accentuate or tie into another in a separate category. All of the above was done to help you readily find pieces that you can mix and match to serve your rehearsal needs.

GETTING STARTED

If you've never tried theatre games before, then take a deep breath and stop worrying. It may seem odd or strange at first. The games may not all work just the way they are supposed to. Your actors may be a little slow to get involved with the initial experimentation, but that's all OK. Start simple. Give everybody plenty of time. Keep encouraging, and before you know it, theatre games will be an indispensable learning tool that everyone will love.

There are only two rules that I ever used in my drama groups while working with theatre games. I found them to be helpful, so I will give them to you.

1. **The director must always be a motivator.** Don't be an iron-fisted Nazi who tears actors limb from limb for repeating their mistakes. Actors learn best through encouragement and challenge, not embarrassment and public criticism.

2. **Everyone must be involved and supportive.** Theatre games don't work unless everyone gets involved. The embarrassment of acting in front of others is lessened when everyone is dealing with the same challenge. A round of applause for everyone's effort goes a long way to create a supportive sense of community.

Our goal with these two rules is to help **create a no-fail environment,** a place where we can learn from our stumbles and be encouraged to try it again.

ACTING MUSCLES

To help your actors better understand the application of theatre games, you might even introduce them to the idea of acting muscles. We all understand how exercising can strengthen our physical muscle structure. Theatre games help us tweak our acting muscles just as well.

Here are a few muscles we can concentrate on:

1. Observation—As actors, we are very much a reflection of the world around us; but before we can reflect it, we must see it. We need to force ourselves out of the scan mode and actually observe and retain what we see passing through our lives.

2. Memory—Our memories are a storehouse of useful acting information. Learning how to tap that valuable resource and strengthen our future retention is very important.

3. Imagination—The wonderful world of make-believe. We've known it from childhood but find it so hard to visit now that we are adults. Imagination is, how ever, a large part of effective acting. Learn to let yourself remember that creative wonderland.

4. Concentration—In today's world of instant access and 30-second sound bytes, concentration and focus can be difficult to maintain. However, an actor's ability to keep things consistent is one of the important building blocks of character development.

THE SIDE COACH

You'll notice throughout the book we keep referring to the side coach. We've even included a definition for it in our Definition of Terms sheet. In case you haven't caught on, the side coach is you. If you are the director or person in charge, all the bits of information for side coach are messages to hopefully help you in your quest.

What is that quest? Well, we are assuming that it's the desire to "find new ways to help your actors find deeper insights and perspectives that will enhance the final theatre communication" (Viola Spolin).

With that in mind, we've included a lot of suggestions that might help you toward that goal.

SO WHAT'S NEXT?

Whether you are a teacher in an acting class, a first-time director of a local drama ministry, someone thinking about starting an improv troupe, or just looking for something different to inject into your rehearsals, the next step is simple. Do it. Experiment with how you can use the games and try variations of your own. I'm certain you will see how fun and stimulating theatre games can be for your actors. At best, your efforts may unlock someone's God-given gifts that are buried under fear and awkwardness. At worst, you may just have a great time. So what's to lose? Enjoy your games.

Bob Hoose

Section 1
TEAM BUILDING

Acting is an ego-oriented, often frightening endeavor. Actors put themselves up in front of others risking failure, humiliation, and perhaps even ridicule. Sounds like fun, huh? Working together with a group of others facing the same challenges and fears can go a long way to help them find support and encouragement in those trying times. Actors need to take chances and even fail if they are going to grow in their skills. What better environment to do that in than with a team of peers that you trust will help pick you up and say, "Not bad."

These team-building games are designed to encourage that sense of trust and support in the group. Most of them will be fairly simple, something anyone can start with and dive into with both feet. We've given you a bunch of them to use in your first few rehearsal periods together or as a simple warm-up or for whenever you think the group needs to rally around one another and revitalize. Now some of the games may seem a little youth-oriented, but don't be fooled. We mature adults like to play like idiots once in a while too. Right?

Invisible Ball

Number of Players: Any number

Objective: To help actors give and take and cultivate imagination and observation (See Invisible Ball [Variation], Change the Object.)

Description: Players sit side by side in a circle. The director shows them an invisible ball. While holding it, the director should stress to them that as they pass this magic ball slowly around the circle, they should keep it the same size, shape, and weight that they have been handed. As each player takes the ball, the director asks questions about its size and motivates the actors to work together and keep what they have been handed consistent. After one pass around the circle, the director can try it again, only this time the ball can change size or weight at the director's command. Again, the actors need to work at slowly passing the ball and sensing its new dimensions as the director verbally changes it.

Side Coach: At first, keep stressing to your actors that broad, fast movements like spinning the ball or bouncing it off their foreheads does not help their fellow actors to see and keep the ball consistent.

"See what is being handed to you."

"Keep it consistent."

"What muscles would you use to lift or carry a ball that weighs that much?"

"Show me someone picking it up and someone letting it go."

Mirror Image

Number of Players: Teams of two

Objective: To strengthen the actor's ability to observe and concentrate. Good icebreaker.

Description: The director has the players pair off in twos, facing each other and standing approximately four feet apart. The players decide who will be PLAYER A and who will be PLAYER B. While looking directly into each other's eyes, they should use their peripheral vision to see all of their partner's movements. PLAYER A initiates a slow, fluid, and random movement, and PLAYER B must mirror the exact movement. After a few moments, the director can call for PLAYER B to take over as the initiator while PLAYER A now follows—all without a break in their movements. Activity and the trading of initiator should continue until the director senses that the players are relaxed and reflecting their partner's movements rather than trying to anticipate them. Additional challenges may include reflecting each other's expressions or increasing the speed of their movements.

Side Coach: The director should stress very slow, fluid movements, especially at first. The slower the movements, the easier it is to reflect them. Also, encourage keeping a mirror between them and not breaking through it.

"Slow and fluid. Give your partner a chance to reflect."

"Think about using full body movements."

"Don't anticipate. Reflect only what you see."

"Switch—don't drop out of it—keep going."

Freeze Tag

Number of Players: Three or more

Objective: To develop teamwork while encouraging trust, creativity, and confidence in improvisation

Description: Two players are chosen and given a relationship and an activity—the Who and the Where. You may use verbal interaction, but this is primarily a physical activity, so no great amount of dialogue is necessary. The players begin acting out their scene. After perhaps 15 to 20 seconds, the director yells, "Freeze." Then another player, chosen from the audience to enter the play area, taps a frozen player on the shoulder and assumes that player's physical position while the original player leaves the playing area. After this has been accomplished, the director will yell, "Begin," and it will be the new player's responsibility to begin a new scene starting from the physical freeze position. A short while into the new scene, the director yells, "Freeze," again and begins the process over with a new player entering the scene.

Example: A scene begins with two prison inmates breaking rocks with a sledgehammer. A few seconds into the scene, the director yells, "Freeze. OK, Renee, go replace someone. Assume that exact position." When the two previous players had frozen, one had his hands raised as if he was about to slam a sledgehammer down on a rock. The other player had just crushed a rock, so his hands were in front of him pointed down toward the ground. Renee taps this second player and assumes his position. The director says, "Think about the position you are in. What could you be doing that's different from the prison guard? Justify your position. Begin."

Renee must begin a new scene with a new activity in a new location. She says, "Could you help me pull in this anchor?" The scene is now in a boat, and the new player, Renee, is pulling in an anchor. The player with his arms in the air must justify his position and begins a fly-casting motion like he's fishing and says, "OK, let me reel in my line, and I'll help you."

Side Coach: You may find it necessary to talk it through with every player the first or second time they try to enter and create a new scene. It sounds difficult, but it's not after a few attempts. Encourage the actors to be very physical and focus primarily on the activity, not the dialogue.

Things to look out for:

1. Actors will want to take their time replacing another player until they can come up with a new activity. Encourage them to jump in, assume the position, and justify the activity.
2. Actors will also want to tell where they are rather than show it. Encourage them just to get involved in an activity and trust that their counterpart will figure it out.

Who Started the Motion?

Number of Players: Any number

Objective: Group cohesion and trust

Description: The director places players in a circle facing inward. One player is chosen and leaves the room. Another player is chosen as leader. He or she will initiate all movements in the circle. All other players are instructed to stare straight ahead but use their peripheral vision to watch for and copy movement changes. The leader inside the circle will clap hands, slap knees, alternate raising arms, and so on. Outside player is brought back in to join the circle and tries to guess who started the movement.

Side Coach: Encourage the players to have instant response to changes around them. Work as a team. Encourage the leader to make changes gradual and not drastic.

Change Three Things

Number of Players: Any number of pairs

Objective: To challenge the actor's skills of observation

Description: The director breaks the players into pairs and has them face each other. He or she can instruct them that they have 30 seconds to observe and remember whatever they can about their partners. At the end of the 30-second period, the players turn their backs to their partners and proceed to make three subtle changes in their appearance. When the director is confident that all the changes have been made, he or she instructs the players to again face each other and observe their partners once more. Each player will get a chance to point out the three changes made.

Example: Changes made should be subtle appearance differences such as buttoning or unbuttoning buttons, rolling up a sleeve, moving or removing jewelry, subtly changing hairstyle (behind ears, etc.).

Side Coach: Point out to the players the importance of training themselves as actors to be observant. Most people, even though they were asked to be observant, will miss one or more of their partner's changes. What does this mean?

"Make your changes subtle. Don't stoop over and drool. Think of how you can change. Make it a challenge."

Change the Object

Number of Players: Any number

Objective: To sharpen the actor's awareness of environment

Description: Players sit in a circle facing each other. The director hands an imaginary object to a player to begin the exercise. That player then takes the object and begins to mold it into another object as if it were a piece of clay—pulling it apart, tearing off pieces to make separate parts, bending it, and/or rolling it out until it has become something totally new. The player then uses the new imaginary object accordingly and passes it to the next player.

Example: The director might hand an actor an imaginary basketball. The player then in turn takes it, smashes it, breaks small pieces off and rolls them out into what might resemble bullets, and then takes the remaining material and forms an imaginary gun. Next, he or she takes the bullets and loads the gun.

Side Coach: Help the actor see that being specific or detailed in the use of space is critical to the actor's and the audience's understanding of the Who, What, and Where of any given scene. The director can also ask the actor receiving the object to use the object before changing it into something else. The director should always encourage the actors to be as specific in their transformations as possible.

Human Machine

Number of Players: Any number

Objective: Creative team building. Relying on others and working together.

Description: A player is chosen to be the first cog or gear in a machine. He or she begins a simple movement that might appear to be a gear or lever-like movement with a body part. In addition, this player adds a sound to his or her movement. One by one players join into the machine, adding their own gear movements and sounds. Players must think creatively and work together with other moving parts, not just by themselves.

Side Coach: The first time through, you may want to limit it to just random gears and switches working together for no specific purpose. The following rounds may be used as a problem-solving exercise as you ask your players to create a specific machine, such as a typewriter or an automobile. The players will have to work together to find and represent the necessary moving parts for each machine. Breaking into smaller groups of players for competition or imposing a time limit may be the next desired step.

Relays

Number of Players: Any number

Objective: To encourage group cohesion and team building through trust and reliance

Description: The director divides players into two or more equal teams of players. The players are to line up as a team, giving themselves space apart from the other teams. Several different types of relays may be played.

Orange Relay—One person from each team puts an orange under his or her chin. When the director begins the game, the players attempt to transfer the orange from the front to the end of the line without using their hands—chins only. If the orange is dropped, it is returned to the first player, then the race continues.

LifeSavers Relay—Each team player puts a toothpick in his or her mouth. The first player in line gets a LifeSaver placed on his or her toothpick. The team attempts to relay the LifeSaver one to another just as in the orange relay with no hands and this time just the use of their toothpicks. If the LifeSaver is dropped, it goes back to PLAYER 1 at the beginning of the line, and play starts over for that team.

Shoe Relay—All players take off both shoes, and all teams place their shoes in a large pile in the middle of the room. The first player from each team runs to the pile, finds, puts on, and ties both of his or her shoes and then runs back to the team and tags the next player, who then runs to the pile. The first team fully shod is the winner.

Crazy Stuff Relay—In this relay, all the teams of players have a separate bag of collected slips and items that they run to, one player at a time. The bags contain slips of paper with silly suggestions and actions written on them. Each player must pull out a slip, perform the requested activity, and then return to the next player in his or her team's line.

Examples: Here are some suggestions for the crazy stuff actions:

1. Perform three front somersaults.
2. Jump on right foot 25 times.
3. Bark like a dog while chasing your tail in a circle three times.
4. Chew this piece of gum and blow a bubble.
5. Sing "Row, Row, Row Your Boat" three times while rowing an imaginary boat on the floor.
6. React as if you just saw a UFO and tell someone about it.

Side Coach: Help keep the players' attention on working together as a team. The competition isn't as important as the activity of working on solving a problem together.

"Learn how to trust one another."

Explosion Tag

Number of Players: Any number

Objective: Simple play as icebreaker and team builder. Encourages creative expression.

Description: This game is much the same as it sounds. One player is chosen as It. The other players need to try to avoid being touched by It. Whenever a player is caught and tagged, he or she "explodes" in his or her most dramatic form and then takes over as It.

Side Coach: Although this is a child's game, it is a very easy way to get actors to break out of a self-conscious shell. Encourage the players to be especially creative in their explosions.

When My Ship Comes In

Number of Players: Any number

Objective: To encourage memory retention

Description: The players all sit in a circle facing each other. One player is elected to begin the exercise. He or she starts by saying, "When my ship comes in, I'm going to take my hat (or any other object)." The next player must repeat what PLAYER 1 has said and add his or her own item. All consecutive players must repeat all the items that have come before in exact order and then add their own. Anyone who fails to remember them all in order must sit back from the circle out of play. Play continues until one player is left. The director may play a second round only adding the challenge of acting out all the items on the list. For example, "Take my shoes." The players will act out putting on their shoes, and so on.

Example:

PLAYER 1: When my ship comes in, I'm going to take my hat.

PLAYER 2: When my ship comes in, I'm going to take my hat and my pillow.

PLAYER 3: When my ship comes in, I'm going to take my hat, my pillow, and my cat.

(And so forth.)

Blind Faith

Number of Players: Four to five players with one key player

Objective: Creating trust among actors and building community

Description: Blindfold one player and place chairs or cubes (four or five) in random places on the stage. After this, the other players should also be placed randomly about the play area. The blindfolded player is then spun around in a circle a few times to disorient him or her. Instruct the blind player to simply start walking. It is the responsibility of the other players to direct the blind player by barely touching him or her so that he or she does not hit a chair or cube. These should be light, gentle touches or taps to signal a change of direction to the blinded player, moving him or her away from the obstacle.

Side Coach: Make sure the players walk at a normal pace. It is OK to begin slow, but instruct them to pick up their pace to normal speed. Help your actors with statements like:

"Walk smoothly, trust the others to guide you."

"OK, pick up your pace now."

"Guide him [her] with just a tap on either shoulder."

Team Mirror

Number of Players: Up to 8 or 10

Objective: To creatively stimulate, warm up, and focus actors (See Mirror Image game.)

Description: Players line up in two opposing V formations. Players in the number one position will be the initiators. The A side will begin the first initiation. The director can switch to the B side after feeling that the players have caught the fluid flow of movements. All players are to mirror the movements of the person facing them. They should also pick up other movements that they may see by occasionally glancing at other players in the group.

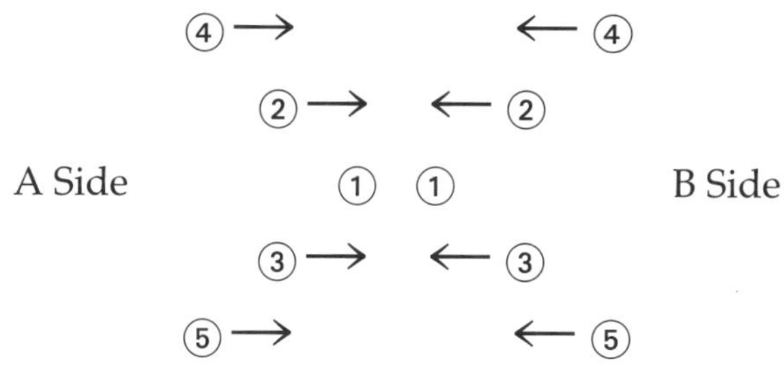

Side Coach: Make sure actors continue to keep their movements slow and fluid. Actors need to remember to mirror the actor directly across from them while occasionally glancing at others near them in the formation. When working, this spontaneous exercise can almost appear to be a rehearsed ballet.

Words-Go-Round

Number of Players: Any number

Objective: General warm-up. To help actors have fun with quick thought and speaking off the top of their heads. Good improv warm-up.

Description: The players all sit in a circle facing each other. The director gets them all started with a slow patty-cake rhythm. First, pat your legs; then clap your hands; then pat the imaginary set of hands in front of you. Because the last pat is an imaginary set of hands, the rhythm will sound like "pat, clap, silence," "pat, clap, silence," and so on. After the slow rhythm is established, the director will say a word in the silence space. The player on his or her right will fill the next silent space with any word that starts with the last letter of the director's inserted word. Each following player keys off the last letter of the previous player's word and adds a new word to the patty-cake rhythm. As the players become comfortable with the pattern, the director can pick up the speed to further challenge them. If a player misses or fumbles with a word, he or she needs just to wait until the next sequence and then add a word.

Example:

Pat, clap, "**d**og"

Pat, clap, "**g**oat"

Pat, clap, "**t**ire"

Pat, clap, "**e**lephant"

Pat, clap, "**t**omorrow"

And so on

Side Coach: Make sure that the rhythm is slow so that the players have time to listen, think, and respond. Don't let them get frustrated. This is to be fun and positive, not threatening. Keep the environment safe and light. Words with a silent vowel, like "rope," can be difficult, but just keep the flow going.

Invisible Ball (Variation)

Number of Players: Any number

Objective: To continue to improve the actors' ability to observe and use their imagination (See Invisible Ball game.)

Description: As with Invisible Ball, the players are placed in a circle. Starting with one ball, the player catches the eye of another player across the circle and bounces the ball to him or her. The director can still change the size and weight of the ball but can also adjust the speed at which the ball travels. The next step is to add an additional ball or balls bouncing in the circle. The director must stress eye contact before bouncing the ball to another player. Another variation would include giving everyone an invisible ball and allowing the entire group to toss the balls against the wall. In this variation, the director should emphasize full use of the players' bodies to keep the balls in motion.

Side Coach: Continue to emphasize concentrating on all the dimensions of the ball or balls, including speed of travel.

"The ball is moving in slow motion, keep the bounce and catch consistent."

"Keep your eye on the ball."

"Now it is a very heavy ball but traveling at a normal speed."

"All right, there are now three balls in the circle. So make sure you have eye contact before you throw."

"Keep each ball consistent and individual."

Transformations

Number of Players: Teams of two

Objective: To help the actors learn to give and take from each other—stimulating trust

Description: The director gives the player an activity and a location—a What and Where. The director assigns a PLAYER 1 and a PLAYER 2 and instructs them to initiate and mirror each other in any simple activity such as jumping jacks. After they reach a natural rhythm in their repeated activity, PLAYER 1 will initiate a gradual change until his or her movement has transformed into a completely different activity. PLAYER 2 will observe the change and continue mirroring. The activity should be very similar in physical movement. It should, in fact, be the similarities between the activities that moves the actors from one to the next. The action continues back and forth through 10 or 12 transformations.

Example: The transformations could go like this:

DIRECTOR: You two are baseball players warming up on a baseball field.

(Activity: The actors begin miming throwing the baseball.)

DIRECTOR: All right, begin your change.

(Activity: PLAYER 1 *begins a slow transformation and keeps throwing and throwing until the motion changes and it appears that he or she is now hammering a nail.* PLAYER 2 *mirrors* PLAYER 1 *until he or she understands what the new activity is. Then that action of hammering will continue until something comes to* PLAYER 2, *who begins a slow transformation until the hammering has slowly transformed into shaking dice and tossing them on the table. So in a matter of a few seconds, you've gone from baseball players, to carpenters, to gamblers, and from the baseball field to a construction site to a casino—all without any dialogue.)*

Side Coach: Make sure actors take their time until they naturally feel the transformation coming on. This is a difficult exercise until the actors get used to the creative transformations, so inject as much creative input as may be needed at first.

"Think about what movement is similar to what you are doing now."

"Take your time, be creative."

"Make the transformation when you feel ready."

One Voice

Number of Players: Four or more

Objective: To instill creative thought while working with others

Description: The director has the players walk randomly throughout the playing area and instructs them to each choose a familiar movement. It could be swinging a bat, throwing a ball, raising a window or any other activity that is familiar. Instruct them as they walk to repeat this simple movement over and over. Once this has been accomplished, the director should instruct the players to add a sound that would be appropriate with their movement. When the players are comfortable with their random walking, familiar movement, and appropriate sound, move to the next step. The director should instruct them to make eye contact with another player and integrate their own movement and sound with the other player's movement and sound. The players can give and take changing all of what they do or combining their movements and sounds with that of the other players' movements and sounds. After this has been completed, you'll have a group of pairs doing similar movements and sounds. They are then to team together until they get eye contact with another pair and the process of blending and give and take begins again. As this process continues, you will notice in most cases a circle will form and all players will be doing a similar movement and sound. Continue on until this is accomplished.

Side Coach: "Stay loose and keep a smooth consistent pace."

"Everyone add a simple movement while walking."

"Now connect with someone else and blend to work together."

Keep an eye out for players that choose too complicated a movement, and encourage them to simplify it.

Walking and Talking

Number of Players: Four or more

Objective: To get actors comfortable with their bodies and voices

Description: The players walk randomly around the playing area without giving attention to other players. They must avoid walking in organized circles or patterns. In the beginning of the exercise, players may stretch, loosen up, or vocalize. When the director feels they are relaxed, he or she should then instruct them to make a change in their movements based on a specific choice of character or environments. The director should offer all the players an A or B choice to choose from.

Examples:

1. You are a politician or a preacher.
2. You are an opera singer or a rap artist.
3. You weigh 5 pounds or 500 pounds.
4. You are on the moon or under water.
5. You are a derelict or a diplomat.

Side Coach: "You are either ______ or ______. Now choose one, go."

"Switch, go."

"Continue walking."

Keep an eye out for those trying to be funny. This exercise is not about words but about relaxed character choices and physical reactions. Encourage players to deal seriously with each adjustment. Make sure actors don't get into conversations with each other. Ask questions like:

"What is the difference between A or B?"

"How does he move differently?"

"How does this different environment affect your movement?"

Section 2
BODY AND MOVEMENT

As stated in the last section, supporting actors to the point of trust and confidence in their acting team will guide and encourage them to take creative risks. That is good. The next logical step is to challenge them in their use of body movement and communication. So much of what an actor presents onstage is made up of physical pictures—pictures that communicate emotions, attitudes, and desires. However, many actors are deficient in those basic movement skills. This set of games can help your actors experiment with all kinds of movement—hopefully encouraging them to make honest, uninhibited use of their bodies as a tool of communication.

Object Movement

Number of Players: Any number

Objective: To help the actors focus on using their bodies to communicate. Good warm-up.

Description: The director instructs the players to react and respond with whatever movement comes to mind when they hear the stimulus word that the director calls out. The director should then call out objects that have different kinds of movements and actions in normal life—sharp movements, smooth movements, loose movements, and twisted movements.

Examples:

Sharp Movements

A. Bucking bronco
B. Cuckoo clock
C. Woodpecker
D. Hammer
E. Typewriter

Smooth Movements

A. Cat
B. Fish
C. Syrup pouring
D. Revolving door
E. Skating

Loose Movements

A. A flag in the breeze
B. A mop
C. Rag doll
D. Clothes on the line
E. Loose sail

Twisted Movements

A. An octopus
B. Pretzel
C. Bulldozer
D. Crumpled paper

Object Movement 2

Number of Players: Any number

Objective: Good warm-up. To help actors connect with their bodies and concentrate. (See Object Movement.)

Description: The director asks all players to react immediately to his or her requests or suggestions. As the director gives the players instructions about items and physical movements, they need to think and react as quickly as possible, become the object, and move the way that object would.

Example:

1. Be a candle standing tall. The candle is lit and burning down to a pool of wax.
2. Be a piece of elastic that is stretched and then released.
3. Be a feather floating on a draft of air and settling to the ground.
4. Be a turtle in his shell who tentatively puts his head and legs out and begins to slowly move.
5. Be a match being struck.
6. Be a forest fire.
7. Be rain.
8. Be a pool of cool water.
9. Be a rushing river.
10. Be a sprinkler.

Pantomimes

Number of Players: One at a time

Objective: To help actors communicate locations, emotions, and intent physically

Description: The director hands out one or more slips of paper with a specific simple scenario on each. The player or players enter the playing area, read the specific scenario, and communicate it to the audience without speaking or making oral sounds. The player must concentrate on showing the Where of the scene as well as what the objective in the scene may be.

Example: Here are some possible scenarios.

1. You want to give the dog a bath but can't keep him in the tub.
2. You want to fix your spouse breakfast but burn the toast.
3. You are on a hike and encounter a bear on a very narrow ledge.
4. You notice money in the storm drain but can't seem to get your hand in to reach it.
5. You need to get to your car parked at the curb after a big snowstorm.
6. You try to iron a shirt, but the iron burns through the material.
7. You are trying to get your scuba license, but the suit they've given you is too small.
8. You are showing off for the ladies at the gym, but you can't lift the weight.
9. You are trying to put a box away in a crowded storage closet but can't get it to fit.
10. You are trying to wrap up a lounge chair as a Christmas present.
11. You want to show your girlfriend that you appreciate her making you a special meal, but the food is terrible.

Join the Environment

Number of Players: Any number

Objective: To help challenge actors to use simple movements to communicate—creative investment

Description: The director selects a player and places him or her in the playing area. The player must choose and demonstrate a simple movement that will suggest to the audience an environment. While PLAYER 1 continues repeating his or her simple movement, other players are invited to join the environment one at a time, demonstrating other simple movements that would be related to or fit into PLAYER 1's environment.

Example: PLAYER 1 chooses to mime swinging a bat. PLAYER 2 decides this would suggest a ball field and becomes the pitcher with a simple overhand throw movement. PLAYER 3 perceives the environment as a city park, so he or she sits on a hillside and begins eating an imaginary sandwich. PLAYER 4 observes all of the above and begins picking up trash in the park, and so on.

Side Coach: Encourage the players that there are no wrong choices. They are only asked to observe what is before them and make a creative choice to join in what they see. At the end of the exercise, the players will have created an interesting tapestry of realistic movement. Ask them how this could fit into stage acting.

"There are no wrong choices here."

"Don't talk about it; do it."

Listening Blind

Number of Players: Four to 10

Objective: To motivate actors to listen and concentrate on their environment while becoming aware of their bodies and their movements

Description: The director blindfolds a player and places him or her approximately 15 to 20 feet away from the other players, all facing him or her and standing in line. The director points to one member of the line. They should raise their hand to acknowledge they understand who was picked. As slowly and quietly as possible, the chosen player walks toward the blind player. Instruct the player that the objective is to get as close as possible without being heard. The blindfolded player is to listen for noises of the approaching player (shoes, clothes rubbing, floor creaking, the player breathing). As the blindfolded player hears noise, he or she is to point toward the noise. The director needs to stand behind the blindfolded player so as to determine if the blindfolded player points correctly. When the blinded player points, the oncoming player freezes until the director can decide whether or not the blinded player was right on mark. If the player has missed, the director says, "No," and play continues. If the oncoming player is caught, then he or she freezes and another player is chosen to approach the blindfolded player.

Side Coach: Make sure the players don't walk too quickly. This exercise is just as much about body control and strategy as it is listening. Make sure the blindfolded player doesn't swing his or her arm around or rapid-fire point. The blindfolded player should be patient and listen for a distinctive noise to discern where its origin is and then point.

How Old Am I?

Number of Players: Four to six

Objective: To explore the subtle differences between different ages

Description: Have the players stand in the playing area in two staggered lines so that all can be seen. The director will instruct the players that he or she will talk them through the exercise. They will all begin the game at the age of two. The players will be allowed to use their physical postures and one word or sound to help signify to the audience that they are the age the director has chosen. The director may choose any age to skip to, but the player's goal is to transform into that age using only their body posture and the same word or sound they started with. The director should challenge the players to explore the differences between differing ages.

Example: A player beginning at age two may choose the word "mama." Then by the time they are 10, it changes to "mom." Then when they are 16, it's "mother," and so on.

Side Coach: "OK, now you are 15 years old. What's the difference between 12 and 15?"

"OK, make the change."

"How does your sound change?"

"What kinds of physical choices show us the difference between 5 and 8 years old?"

"How about 8 and 12 years old?"

What's Beyond?

Number of Players: One

Objective: To effectively utilize acting space and experiment with emotional and physical expression

Description: The player is instructed to decide on some event that is about to happen. He or she should then enter the playing area, utilizing the space (furniture, doors, windows, etc.) and behaving in a manner appropriate to the event that is about to take place. No dialogue may be used. When the player is finished, ask the audience what it is that is going to happen next. The player should keep it to himself or herself, and if the class doesn't guess correctly, the player should continue or begin again, this time being more specific.

Examples:

1. Checking yourself in the mirror before walking out to be married.
2. A child expecting to be spanked.
3. A wife waiting anxiously for her husband to return home in a big storm.

Side Coach: "What can you do to make it clearer?"

"What made that confusing?"

"Be as specific as possible."

Past/Present/Future

Number of Players: One or more

Objective: To utilize stage space. Strengthen nonverbal physical communication. (See What's Beyond?)

Description: This is a variation of What's Beyond? The player is instructed that the playing area represents the present. As the player enters the playing area (present), he or she should not only behave in a manner that would suggest where he or she is, but also where he or she has just come from (past). After the player feels he or she has established the present, the player should exit (future) in a way that would suggest where he or she is going. No dialogue may be used. After the player completes the exercise, the director can ask the class what they perceived was the past, present, and future of the scene and how it could be made clearer.

Example:

1. By entering, the player shows us where he or she has been. The player enters as if on ice skates—mimes taking off shin guards and a mask. We know the player was ice skating/playing hockey (past).
2. When the player opens what appears to be a locker and hangs his or her gear in the locker, this establishes the locker room (present).
3. Then the player walks to another location onstage, mimes opening a door, and reaches inside and mimes turning on a shower. We now know he or she is going into a shower (future).

Follow the Leader

Number of Players: Two to four

Objective: To help actors justify stage movements and work with their stage area. To encourage listening and responding.

Description: Assign the players an acting order (1, 2, 3, 4 or A, B, C, D). They can then only move in this order. The director places the scene in a location where a wide variety of imaginary utensils or set pieces might be available (i.e., kitchen, pool hall, office copy room, weight room). After the Where of the scene is established, the director gives the players a relationship (i.e., cooks, frat buddies, secretaries). As the scene begins, PLAYER 1 will move to do something in the scene. The other players will then have to justify one by one joining the scene in the same area as PLAYER 1. They can only enter the scene in the order they were originally chosen. When all the players have entered the scene, then PLAYER 1 moves again, and follow the leader continues with each player constantly justifying through words and actions why he or she has followed.

Example: Suppose you have chosen the Where to be a kitchen and the Who to be cooks. The dialogue and movement might be as follows:

PLAYER 1: Well, I'm going to heat up the grill so we can get breakfast going. *(Moves to an area on the stage and mimes turning on the grill)*

PLAYER 2 *(mimes grabbing something from a shelf)*: Here, let me bring you the pancake mix. *(Follows* PLAYER 1)

PLAYER 3 *(mimes taking something out of a drawer)*: Here, you guys, use these new spatulas. *(Takes the objects to them)*

PLAYER 4: You are making such a mess. *(Mimes grabbing a mop and follows the group over to the grill and begins mopping at their feet)* There.

It is then PLAYER 1's turn to justify going to another location, and the process begins again.

Side Coach: Make sure the scene continues on and the movements merely tie the scene together. The scene is not about movement but about creative ways to make the scene work better.

"Don't rush. Think your way to the next move."

"Be patient. Help each other out."

"It doesn't matter how quickly you follow; just justify the movement."

Add an Object

Number of Players: Five to 10

Objective: To teach actors how to creatively use their playing space. Motivates actors to observe and remember.

Description: Seat the players facing the playing area with an unobstructed view. The key to the success of this game is the ability of the players to see and remember all that is done by each individual player. Number the players off (1 to 10). PLAYER 1 will have the responsibility to decide the Where that the acting space will represent—whether it is a kitchen, bathroom, living room, or some other location. PLAYER 1, without verbalizing the Where, will then enter the playing area, use one imaginary object and then exit the space. PLAYER 2 then enters and uses the same object No. 1 used, then adds the use of another imaginary object. Each following player must use all of the objects used before and add another one. The players should be encouraged to use the objects differently and in as many creative ways as possible. The Where of the scene may change based on each player's observation of what has been done previously or based on what object each new player introduces. Play ends when a player can't remember the objects previously used or when the director stops the scene.

Example: PLAYER 1 enters the scene, turns on a sink faucet, and exits.

PLAYER 2 enters, rinses hands under the water, adds his or her own object (soap), and then turns off the faucet and exits.

PLAYER 3 enters, turns on the faucet, uses the soap, and adds drying his or her hands on a towel. Up to this point, the actors may have all seen the scene as taking place in a bathroom.

PLAYER 4, however, enters, washes his or her face with soap and water, turns off the faucet, dries his or her face on the towel, then opens the refrigerator door and exits. With one added use of an object, our bathroom becomes a kitchen. Play continues with as many creative variations as the players let themselves accomplish.

Side Coach: It will be the tendency for players to add more than one object. If this happens, make sure the player goes back and eliminates one of the added objects. You may want the player to retrace his or her movements, adding only one object this time. Explain to the players at the top of the exercise the difference between one or two objects. A sink with water is one object, but a sink and a bar of soap are two. A toilet has a lid, tank top, and a flusher; all are one object, but toilet paper is a second object. The director can also ask players questions like:

"What was unclear?"

"What was clear?"

"How could we make it more clear?"

The director should also notice and point out things like:

1. Did the trash can keep moving?
2. Did the towels keep changing sizes?
3. Did the cabinets change height?
4. Did doors open or close differently?

After clearing up these questions or inconsistencies, play could begin again, perhaps starting with the last player from the previous game and working backward. The director might also stress where the actors are coming from, where they are, and where they are going. (See Past/Present/Future.)

Touchy Topic

Number of Players: Two to four

Objective: To encourage listening, natural physical give and take, and honest character interaction between actors

Description: The director chooses a topic of conversation for the players. The players may then choose the Who (their relationship) and the Where (location) of the scene. The players' choices must allow physical contact in normal activity. The players are then to interact with each other in normal activity but may only talk when they make physical contact. One player may initiate a conversation by touching first then speaking. Either player may speak during contact, but if the physical contact breaks midsentence, they both must stop speaking while they continue physical space work. When they are able to come into physical contact with one another, someone may speak again.

Players need to keep several things in mind:

1. The topic of conversation.
2. Normal physical interaction in the specific location.
3. Not to hold the physical contact longer than would be natural.
4. To explore ways of touching without using just their hands.

Explore ways of touching given their relationship, occupation, and topic.

Example: Suppose the relationship is between a father and a son. The father might place his hand on the son's shoulder to give him fatherly advice and then take it off when he is finished. The son would then have to find a way to touch his dad and talk.

Side Coach: "You've kept contact a little too long. Break contact and keep thinking."

"What can you reasonably be doing while no one is talking?"

"How do you keep communicating after the contact has been broken?"

Section 3
SPONTANEITY

As we enter into the realm of both physical and verbal improvisation, we encounter that dank, dark terror of having to walk, talk, and perhaps even chew gum at the same time. So often actors hate improvisation because they feel that their brains just don't work fast enough to keep up with it all. Not true. In actuality, our brains work with a-fraction-of-a-second swiftness. The problem is that we all have conditioned ourselves to overthink everything. We consider and reconsider everything we're about to say in order to come up with just the right words. That may work very well when asking a pretty girl for a date or your boss for a raise, but it is a killer in improvisation. Improvisation demands fluid, honest, off-the-top-of-your-head response to work at its best. The benefit to your acting will far outweigh the inconvenience of having to reprogram yourself to spontaneous reaction. For one thing, improvisation encourages a freedom of thought and easy interaction that makes creative choices onstage (both verbal and physical) almost easy. This next set of exercises is designed to help kick start your actors' natural ability to think freely and respond quickly. You'll see—reprogramming isn't all that tough after all.

Expert

Number of Players: One

Objective: A good confidence builder for the actor who struggles with self-trust

Description: The director chooses and places a player alone in a chair or stool onstage and instructs the player that he or she is an expert on any given topic. It does not need to be a topic that the player is familiar with; in fact, it often works better if the player knows nothing of the topic. When the players are somewhat familiar with their topic, they become too literal and it works against the exercise. The director instructs the player that everything he or she answers is correct. After all, an expert knows more than anyone about this topic. The rest of the audience then asks questions of the expert. Answers must be immediate and without pause or deep, searching thought. An expert would know the answer.

Side Coach: Make sure the players don't cheat. Most players will try to stall or avoid answering the question long enough for them to think of a clever answer. They might say things like, "Oh, I'm glad you asked that" or "In my expert opinion," in which case you can encourage them to stop stalling and please give an instant answer. The humor in this exercise will come out of the immediacy of the answers and the assuredness with which the actor answers questions he or she knows nothing about.

Firing Line

Number of Players: Four to six

Objective: To help actors overcome the fear of speaking without a script. This is an easy intro to improvisation.

Description: One player is placed in a chair or on a stool facing the remaining three to five players standing in a line. The players in line will throw a word at the seated player, one at a time. The words should be unrelated. The seated player will respond to the word with the first related word that comes to mind. The director can encourage the players to give and take spontaneously without pause, creating a rhythm back and forth. After the players settle into this back-and-forth rhythm, the director can then ask the players to try to relate on both sides of the firing line. New players can be rotated in and out of the chair until each have had a chance to be fired upon.

Example:

PLAYER A says, "Sky."

CHAIR PLAYER says, "Blue," since blue would be related to sky.

PLAYER B says, "Dog."

CHAIR PLAYER says, "Cat."

PLAYER C says, "Eat."

CHAIR PLAYER says, "Food," and so on.

With variation, both sides must be related.

PLAYER A says, "Tree."

CHAIR PLAYER says, "Green."

PLAYER B has to say a word related to green and says "Blue."

CHAIR PLAYER says, "Sky."

PLAYER C says, "Birds."

CHAIR PLAYER says, "Egg," and so on—each side relating to the other.

Side Coach: This game needs to be rapid and encourage players to trust themselves and just respond. They don't need to come up with the best word, just the first thing that comes to mind. The idea is to stop the brain from the hang-up of trying to think before responding.

Expert Panel

Number of Players: Three or four

Objective: To build trust and confidence in a team. Strengthen creativity and imagination. (See Expert.)

Description: This game plays exactly like the Expert only with a team of players. The director chooses three or more players who are placed in the playing area. The audience chooses an area of expertise for them all. Players will actually become experts on different aspects of the same topic. The players need know nothing about the topic in reality. In fact, it is usually more interesting if they don't have any prior knowledge of the subject. The audience then asks them questions about their topic of expertise at random. The audience may direct their questions at a certain individual player or at the panel in general. The panel's goal is to, without stalling, answer the question as quickly and forthrightly as possible. With the panel, however, they have the added advantage of being able to help each other out and keep the discussion brisk and fresh.

Side Coach: The players usually find the most success when they answer with the first thought that comes to mind.

Expert Gibberish

Number of Players: One

Objective: To strengthen memory recall, time awareness, and creativity. The exercise can also be helpful when making logical character choices or working on believable foreign characters.

Description: Have a player sit on the playing area as in the Expert exercise. Instruct the player that in round one, he or she is to explain in one minute how something works or how to perform a particular activity. The player should be instructed to remember all he or she says in order to repeat it later. When the player has finished, the director can tell how long the exercise took and ask him or her to try to repeat it, getting as close to one minute as possible.

Here is a step-by-step of round one:

1. Describe an activity in one minute.
2. Time the player.
3. Ask the player how long he or she took.
4. Tell the player the actual time.
5. Ask the player to repeat, remembering as much as possible and keeping it as close to one minute as possible.

In round two, the player is to repeat the above activity description in close to one minute, but this time the words will be replaced with foreign gibberish. The audience must see the explanation and understand it the second round as clearly as the first. Encourage the players to take advantage of their physicality in the description, using similar sounds. At the end of this round, the audience can discuss what they did or did not see the second round through.

Example: Here are some suggestions for expert activities.

1. How does a CD work?
2. How does sunblock work?
3. How do you bake a cake?
4. How does the digestive system work?
5. How do you disassemble an M16 rifle?

Object Objective

Number of Players: One

Objective: To encourage creative spontaneity. To encourage use of props and set pieces.

Description: The director lays five objects of choice on a table. Larger objects may be used but must be readily at hand for the player. The player is then instructed to step into the environment and use the five objects to play out an impromptu scene or tell a story. The objects can help the player make his or her way through the story or may be used as some kind of physical example. The player, however, uses all the objects at some point.

Example: Tell us about your day today using these five unrelated objects.

1. A golf ball
2. A scarf
3. A cup
4. A pencil
5. A book

Side Coach: "Don't worry about thinking up some funny story. Just use the objects."

"Tell us what really happened today. Just tie these things into it."

"Can you use the objects as examples of something?"

"Can they help us see part of your story?"

Let's Get Physical

Number of Players: Three

Objective: To encourage good listening and observation skills. Learning how to break through physical barriers and stiffness.

Description: Three players are chosen, and one is asked to temporarily leave the room. The director then receives suggestions for three activities. He or she instructs the two remaining players that they must somehow get the returning actor to join into their scene and act out the three activities without actually verbally saying what the activities are. The two players may give PLAYER 1 clues through their dialogue and interaction but may not tell PLAYER 1 what to do. The returning player's only task is to observe, listen, and do, do, do. Everything the player hears, he or she should try to attach to a physical activity. When PLAYER 1 completes an activity, the audience must applaud or cheer to let him or her know to move on to the next one. Play ends when all three activities are accomplished.

Examples: Physical activities can include:

1. Brushing your teeth
2. Digging a ditch
3. Walking the dog
4. Changing the lightbulb
5. Taking a bath

One of the principal players may say, "Oh, hi, I'm glad you came to the party." PLAYER 1 could start blowing up balloons, blowing party horns, anything that could be related to the clue party.

Side Coach: Keep the players focused on helping PLAYER 1 discover the desired activities. When the scene is over, PLAYER 1 should probably be exhausted.

Two Conversations

Number of Players: Three

Objective: To encourage actors to listen and respond to others in a scene

Description: The director assigns a different topic of conversation to two of three players. The two players are then asked to stand on the left and right of the third player. The outside players are then told to simultaneously talk about their topics to the player in the middle. The center player must listen to both conversations at the same time and ping-pong back and forth between them, attempting to carry on a conversation with both at the same time. The center player should be constantly going back and forth, listening for a few seconds to one and briefly answering and then listening to the other and briefly answering. Rotate your players around so that everyone has a chance to play the center position.

Side Coach: Make sure that the outside players are oblivious to the other outside player. They need to focus on the center player and their conversation only. Be sure the center player is not just answering with yes and no but is really hearing and answering the conversations appropriately. Also make sure that the center player is giving equal attention to each conversation.

Radio

Number of Players: Four or more

Objective: To create flexibility in your actors. To familiarize them with things that may be foreign to them.

Description: Line up your players facing the director. The players are each assigned a different type of radio program. They must use all the different elements of each radio station from style of announcer to style of music or conversation. The director will point randomly to each player, one at a time. The player becomes the voice of that station, then stops and remains quiet while other players are chosen. The overall affect will be of changing the frequency dial on the radio and listening to a variety of stations. The director must also instruct the players not to repeat or continue a song but to begin a new segment each time he or she is pointed to. Play should continue until the players are performing easily. Start the game again, switching stations among the players. Lastly, try the exercise again letting the players choose their own stations.

Examples:

1. Rock
2. Easy listening
3. Talk radio
4. Christian contemporary
5. Gospel
6. Sports
7. Country
8. Classical
9. Classic rock
10. Educational
11. Jazz

Ins and Outs

Number of Players: Two

Objective: To help actors make and justify creative choices onstage. To reemphasize the importance of strong entrances and exits.

Description: The director will place two players in the playing area with a Who, Where, and What for the scene. The players are then instructed to make and justify as many entrances and exits in the course of their scene as possible. They need to use their imaginations to create as many exits and reasons for exiting and coming back in as possible. The director can encourage and side coach them as the game progresses.

Example: Two cooks in a kitchen. The dinner they are preparing is for the president and must be prepared quickly and to perfection. Going to the freezer and back may be one move. Then perhaps the other cook notices that the overhead exhaust fan has stopped. He or she must exit and bring in a ladder to reach it. The space becomes an ever-changing space with as many doors, windows, cabinets, and closets as the players require.

Side Coach: Encourage the players to use their imagination. No wrong choices here except that they should not repeat the same exits. Don't go to the bathroom, storeroom, or kitchen twice. This exercise can be exhausting but helps actors get used to thinking offstage as well as onstage.

Return Department

Number of Players: Four to six

Objective: To challenge an actor's improvisational interaction, observation skills, and physical communication

Description: One player is chosen and asked to leave the room temporarily. Three or more players are chosen to assist PLAYER 1 upon his or her return. The scene is a return department. The director explains PLAYER 1 will be returning a purchased item, but when entering the scene, he or she will be unaware of what that item is. The audience is asked to now suggest what PLAYER 1 is returning. They should suggest an interesting, perhaps hard-to-find item as well as a substance that the item can be filled with. The other chosen players now enter the playing area. PLAYER 2 will be the return department manager standing at the return window. The remaining players will actually be there to assist PLAYER 1. They will use silent mime and simple movements to help communicate the identity of the returned item and its contents to PLAYER 1. The challenge to PLAYER 1 is to enter the scene, explain to the manager the reason for returning the purchased item, and at the same time try to figure out (based on the helpers' mimed actions) what he or she actually has and what it is filled with. As the player guesses and covers up mistakes, he or she is rewarded with cheers or boos from the audience based on his or her accuracy.

Example:

(PLAYER 1 *exits the room. The audience decides that the item to be returned is a fishbowl filled with peanut butter.* PLAYER 2 *takes place behind the return window.* PLAYERS 3 *and* 4 *will stand behind him or her so that* PLAYER 1 *can get a clear view of them.* PLAYER 1 *enters the scene carrying something.)*

PLAYER 2: Can I help you.

PLAYER 1: Yes, I'd like to return this . . . thing.

(Meanwhile, PLAYERS 3 *and* 4 *are miming swimming like a fish.)*

PLAYER 2: Just for the paperwork, what is that thing?

PLAYER 1: It's a fish.

AUDIENCE: Boo.

PLAYER 1: That is, it's a fishy sort of thing.

(The audience applauds.)

PLAYER 2: Yes, it is sort of fishy, isn't it?

(PLAYERS 3 *and* 4 *are miming fish and bowling now, and so on.)*

Side Coach: Even though this may sound very difficult, it isn't. It's a challenging game that throws a lot of responsibility to all the players. PLAYER 2 must be ready to subtly help PLAYER 1 find the answers while keeping the scene moving ahead. PLAYERS 3 and 4 must be ready to abandon something that isn't working and jump into another activity quickly. They must always be thinking of the next way they can help PLAYER 1.

"OK, No. 1, keep the scene moving, but be ready to cover your mistakes if necessary."

"No. 3, that's not working. What else could get the picture across?"

Translations

Number of Players: Three

Objective: To help actors listen and respond while stimulating their improv creativity (See Foreign Exchange.)

Description: Seat three players in chairs facing the audience. The two on the outside will speak in gibberish. The player in the center will translate for them. The director, with help from the audience, can set up a scenario like a marriage counselor's office or just come up with a topic of conversation for the two to talk gibberish about. PLAYER 1 will make a statement in gibberish. The TRANSLATOR will listen and translate what PLAYER 1 has said. Then PLAYER 2 will answer in gibberish. The variation in this game is that although the gibberish should not make sense, the director should encourage the TRANSLATOR to use the sounds of the gibberish to aid in the translation.

Example:

PLAYER 1: Yo may mo boh doh hot.

TRANSLATOR: You make my body hurt.

After the players reach a point of fluid interaction, the director can rotate the players until all have had the opportunity to play each role.

Side Coach: Make sure players wait for the translation before speaking. Make sure the players are using the sounds of the gibberish to come up with their story.

Section 4
GIVE AND TAKE

Continuing on with the theme of natural response and easy interaction onstage, we come to Give and Take. This set of exercises takes us to the next level of challenge, encouraging the actor to listen and respond, to watch and react, and all within the confines of typical scene work. The exercises are a bit more difficult in spots but tons of fun.

Oh Yeah

Number of Players: Two

Objective: To help actors focus on achieving goals and working on verbal confidence over physical

Description: The director places two players knee-to-knee facing each other. The audience is asked for two topic suggestions. The topics may be totally unrelated. The players will be instructed to try to convince the opposing player that their point of view on the given topic is correct. Even though the topics are unrelated, the two players will still push forward to achieve their goals. The two conversations are to run simultaneously. This will improve listening and force the players to play off what the other player is saying but stay on task and push toward their separate goals.

Example: PLAYER 1 did better than PLAYER 2 on a driving test. Her goal is to get PLAYER 2 to admit that she is a better driver. PLAYER 2, on the other hand, is trying to convince PLAYER 1 to marry him.

Side Coach: Don't let the players pause or lose focus of their individual goals. Keep them driving forward. This can be an effective exercise for scene work in a play if you want to help actors get their objectives clear and focused.

Embellish

Number of Players: Two

Objective: Encourages actors to listen to one another and motivates the positive interactive qualities of improvisation

Description: The director places two players face-to-face and gives them a simple sentence to begin with. The players are then instructed to repeat that sentence back and forth and add one descriptive word each time they say it.

Example:

DIRECTOR: The sentence is, "The dog chased the cat."

PLAYER 1: The dog chased the cat.

PLAYER 2: The dog chased the yellow cat.

PLAYER 1: The big dog chased the yellow cat.

PLAYER 2: The big, shaggy dog chased the yellow cat.

PLAYER 1: The big, shaggy dog chased the yellow cat Sunday.

(And so on.)

Side Coach: This is a simple exercise that can be helpful to actors who are afraid of using their words. It encourages actually listening and responding to each other.

Camera

Number of Players: Two

Objective: To instill a sense of living in an environment. Motivating truthful interaction between characters.

Description: The director places two players in the playing area, giving them a relationship, a location, and an activity/conflict that they must work on—the Who, Where, and What. The improv then continues on its own with the two actors interacting with each other. The players may not look directly at each other, however, unless the director gives them permission to do so. The director will utilize four commands: camera (which directs both players to look at each other), no camera (which directs the players to look anywhere else but at each other), PLAYER 1 camera (which directs PLAYER 1 only to look at his or her counterpart), PLAYER 2 camera (which directs PLAYER 2 to look at his or her counterpart). The director may alternate these commands in the course of the improv as seen fit. The goal is to challenge the actors to find ways to communicate with and without eye contact while listening, responding, and using their surroundings.

Example:

1. Give the players a relationship (husband and wife, boss and secretary, neighbors).
2. Give them a location for the scene (a restaurant, an office building, bathroom, over the backyard fence).
3. Give them an activity/conflict (redecorating, finishing a last-minute report, arguing over a neighbor's disobedient pet).

Begin the scene with camera or no camera and have fun.

Side Coach: Keep in mind that some actors will find it difficult to speak to someone without eye contact while others will find just the opposite to be true. However, in real life, we communicate while performing other tasks that demand our focus or attention all the time. You may have to go back to no camera more often than not, but concentrate on forcing your actors to live within their environment and create activities that will in turn create dialogue.

Two Topics

Number of Players: Three

Objective: To encourage actors to listen and be aware of the world around them in their playing area (See Two Conversations.)

Description: The director places three players in the playing area. The two outside players will both be given a magazine or newspaper. The director instructs the outside players to read a paragraph or two from their newspapers at the same time. The center player just listens. After the paragraphs are read aloud, the center player is asked to tell all he or she can remember about the two topics.

Side Coach: This can be an embarrassing exercise if not set up as simply an exercise. This is just to strengthen acting muscles.

Alter Ego

Number of Players: Four

Objective: A good transition exercise into improvisational work. Encourages good listening skills and a quick response. (See Foreign Exchange, Translations.)

Description: The director chooses four players. PLAYERS 1 and 2 are given a relationship, a location for the scene, and a conflict that the two of them are trying to resolve. PLAYER 3 is then assigned to PLAYER 1 and PLAYER 4 is assigned to PLAYER 2 as their alter egos. Every time PLAYER 1 says something to PLAYER 2, PLAYER 3 will reveal to us verbally what's really on PLAYER 1's mind. PLAYER 4 will do the same for PLAYER 2. PLAYERS 3 and 4 will really be revealing for us a second conversation that PLAYERS 1 and 2 are having but not speaking. As the scene continues and the director sees that the actors are responding comfortably, he or she may decide to switch the roles and make PLAYERS 3 and 4 our central characters with PLAYERS 1 and 2 taking the role of alter ego.

Example: The relationships could be coworkers. A location could be a company cafeteria, and the conflict could be the upcoming promotion list.

PLAYER 1 (FRED): Hey there, good buddy.

PLAYER 3 (ALTER EGO): You back-stabbing, job-stealing weasel.

PLAYER 2 (JOHN): Oh, hi, Fred.

PLAYER 4 (ALTER EGO): Not here, Fred. There are a million tables.

PLAYER 1 (FRED): My, my, meat loaf again, huh, John? My favorite.

PLAYER 3 (ALTER EGO): Doesn't your wife know how to make anything else, you poor sap?

Side Coach: Encourage the players that the key to success is listening closely before adding information.

One and Two Word Story

Number of Players: Four to 10

Objective: To encourage actors to listen and respond creatively. A good beginning exercise developing skills needed for improvisation.

Description: The director lines the players up side by side and asks them to tell us a story with each player adding two words at a time. The first round of this game may be accomplished with only one pass down and back through the line of players. If there are 5 players, the play would start with PLAYER 1. PLAYER 1 begins the story with its first two words, then play proceeds with each player adding two words. Once PLAYER 5 has added two words, the play proceeds back through PLAYERS 4, 3, 2, and ends with PLAYER 1's last two words. With that few players, the story will, of course, be very short. The goal is not a long or even a very interesting story but one that simply makes sense. The director can try this approach a time or two to make sure the players understand and are comfortable with the game. In round No. 2, the players can be given a chance to tell a story using as many passes up and down the line as they desire, but this time limited to only one word per player. To help guide the players, the director may even come up with a title to the story before they begin. This will give the players a goal to shoot for or a bit of information to use as creative fodder. Play can continue with a number of further rounds if the director thinks the players are comfortable and looking for a greater challenge. The director can expand each player's input to one sentence or perhaps to a full paragraph. Another round would include having other players or volunteers from the audience act out the story following the directions of the storytellers. The key to acting out the story would be to not only duplicate the actions of the characters but also become and mime the objects of the story (horses, gates, mountains, chairs, etc.).

Side Coach: Try to remind the players that action words and descriptive words (adverbs and adjectives) will help move the story along. Also encourage the players to remember all the characters and elements that have been introduced in the story. All the story's elements must be reincorporated and tied up before the story may end. If you decide to have someone act out the story, encourage the storytellers to focus their action around one central character. Get that character into trouble, get him or her out of trouble, and end the story—begin, middle, and end. After the end, perhaps the storytellers can come up with a moral to the story, one or two words at a time.

Example:

PLAYER 1: One day

PLAYER 2: a dog

PLAYER 3: bit a

PLAYER 4: ice cream

PLAYER 5: truck. He

PLAYER 6: ate right

PLAYER 7: through to

PLAYER 8: the creamy

PLAYER 9: center, and

PLAYER 10: he belched.

(End of story)

Starting Line/Finish Line

Number of Players: Two

Objective: To encourage actors to think on their feet, listen and respond with other actors, and rely on each other for creativity and support

Description: The director sets up the basic ground rules of an improvisation with the two players—the Who, What, and Where of the scene that the two must deal with. On top of these elements, the players must work with two unrelated lines suggested by the audience. The first line suggested will be the line that begins the scene. Either player may use it, and then play proceeds. The players then interact and work their way to the point where they can incorporate the second suggested line into the scene. When the second line is used, the scene is over.

Example: The director sets up the scene with, "The two of you are brother and sister. You are at her apartment. The brother has come over to tell his sister that he has wrecked her car that he borrowed."

The two suggested lines are:

1. Where's my hankie?
2. I caught five fish with that rod and reel.

The scene may go like this:

(BROTHER *knocks at the door.* SISTER *opens the door but is looking oddly and squinting one eye.)*

SISTER: Where's my hankie?

BROTHER: What?

SISTER: I think I've got something in my eye. Oh, sorry, come on in, Brad.

BROTHER: Thanks, Sis. Can I help? You know how I would bend over backward for you anytime.

(And so on.)

Side Coach: Make sure the two lines are not related to each other or the relationship of the players. Also, make sure the players remember their relationship and where they are. It might be a good idea to have the players repeat the two lines into memory or have them written on a chalkboard before starting the scene.

Dubbing

Number of Players: Four to six

Objective: To break free of an actor's speech and movement patterns. To help actors rely on one another. (See Alter Ego.)

Description: Two or three players are chosen for Team A and two or three players (same sexes as Team A) will be chosen to be their voices. The director can decide, with the help of the audience, what the relationships of Team A should be, where the scene takes place, and what conflict or desire they will all be dealing with. The scene is then acted out with Team A interacting physically but Team B speaking the lines. Team A will silently move their mouths but not try to mouth any specific words. Both teams of players will be following each other—awkwardly at first and eventually get close to working as one set of players. After about 10 minutes of play, the director can have the teams switch places and continue the same scene or choose a new one.

Foreign Exchange

Number of Players: Four

Objective: To aid the actor along the path toward an honest give-and-take unscripted conversation

Description: Four players are chosen. Two of the players are given an interactive relationship by the director (a blind date usually works well). These two players are seated. The audience may offer a location where their activity takes place (drive-in, restaurant, park). Then the director instructs the seated players that they both speak a different foreign language and must speak to each other in gibberish. The other two players are assigned the duty of standing behind the two central players and interpreting or translating everything they say in gibberish into English. The seated players communicate with each other about any given topic they choose (i.e., the menu, their home countries, the movie) using both inflection and body language to communicate their meaning. The interpreters will observe all the clues from the seated players and interpret as they see fit. The seated players must, of course, respond to one another only after they have heard the English interpretation. Their reactions to each other will be affected by the interpretation, whether it was what they intend to say or not. The director can let play flow until the players establish a fluid give and take and then have the players switch roles.

Example:

DIRECTOR: PLAYERS 1 and 2 are on a first date at McDonald's. Both are from different countries, so their interpreters will interpret for them. Begin.

PLAYER 1: Ya ba da ba do oo be la la.

PLAYER 3: Your eyes are beautiful over these Chicken McNuggets.

PLAYER 2: Yabinsky binsky hicklinsky pooh.

PLAYER 4: You have a piece of lettuce between your teeth.

(And so on.)

Side Coach: Make sure the seated actors relate only to each other and not to their interpreters. The interpreters are simply their voices. Encourage various examples of foreign gibberish—French gibberish, German gibberish, Asian gibberish.

Table Talk Tag

Number of Players: Four

Objective: To encourage give and take between actors. To loosen up an actor's creative thought and speed up response time.

Description: Four players are chosen and placed at two adjoining tables. The director establishes the improvisational groundwork for the scene—the Who, What, and Where. The two separate couples will have two separate and unrelated conversations. In this exercise, however, the couples are to listen to the other couple's conversation, using their last word or words to influence the next couple's conversation. The players will give and take between the two tables, never relating to the other table's conversation, just keying off their last words.

Example:

(Two married couples in a famous restaurant. Table A's conflict is the food. Table B's conflict is politics.)

TABLE A MAN: I can't believe they charged that much for that tiny salad.

TABLE A WOMAN: Oh, but it is my favorite. It's hearts of romaine with herb dressing.

TABLE B MAN: Herb Idolston. I can't believe he got elected.

TABLE B WOMAN: Well, the Republicans won everything else, which was very sweet.

TABLE A MAN: It's always been too sweet for me.

TABLE A WOMAN: Well, you know my sweet tooth.

TABLE B MAN: Yeah, those Democrats were fighting tooth and nail to keep control of the Senate.

TABLE B WOMAN: That and the House.

TABLE A MAN: Well, just give me a simple house salad, I say, and a simple price.

TABLE A WOMAN: You are such a tightwad. Enjoy.

(And so on.)

Side Coach: Keep the players on their own conflict. Don't let them wander off into boring chatter. The scene must be central with the added challenge of playing off key words. Help your actors see how this kind of listening and freedom of thought can help them onstage.

Dubbing/Foreign Movie

Number of Players: Four to six

Objective: To encourage creative thought and spontaneous interaction (See Dubbing and Foreign Exchange)

Description: As in Dubbing, two or three players are chosen for Team A and the same number for Team B. Team B will be Team A's voices. This time, however, the director and the audience decide on a movie title, a language for this movie (French, Italian, Japanese, etc.), and a style of movie (science fiction, western, spy, horror, etc.). Team A will be the stars of the picture and will act out a scene based upon the above choices. Team B will designate who translates for whom in Team A, and will translate each line spoken in the course of the movie. The players in Team A will freeze after each spoken line until the proper interpretation is given. Team B must obviously be quick in their translations. The scene will end up being a give and take between Team A's actions and Team B's voices.

Example: Our movie title might be "Creatures from the Black Heart of the Seven Hills." It's a Japanese film, and the style is a western.

Side Coach: Keep the players on track. Help Team A to physically interact as well as listen and respond to the interpretations. The quicker the give and take, the more smoothly the exercise will proceed.

Starting Line/Finish Line
(Relay)

Number of Players: Two to 10

Objective: To encourage actors to rely on one another and think quickly on their feet—creative investment (See Starting Line / Finish Line.)

Description: The set-up for this game is essentially the same as Starting Line / Finish Line. The director starts with a relationship, a location, and a conflict. Two players begin the play. This time, however, there are multiple unrelated lines suggested by the audience. The number of lines you use will depend on how long you want the exercise to last. PLAYER A will say the first line, beginning the scene. The scene proceeds until PLAYER B ends the scene with the second suggested line. The players freeze. PLAYER A exits the playing area, and PLAYER C joins PLAYER B. PLAYER B begins the next scene with the same line the previous scene just ended with. The new scene continues, changing characters, relationships, location—whatever the actors choose at the moment—until PLAYER C ends it with the third suggested line. The players freeze. PLAYER B exits, and PLAYER D enters and joins PLAYER C on the playing area. PLAYER C begins the next scene with the same line the previous scene just ended with. The play continues in this tag-team fashion until PLAYER A once again enters the playing area and ends the last scene with the same line he or she began the first scene with.

Example: Five unrelated lines might be:

1. Where is my hankie?
2. I caught five fish with that rod and reel.
3. Go ahead, make my day.
4. If you don't eat your crusts, no dessert.
5. Don't do that; he's my father.

The first scene will begin with line one, and the last scene will end with line one.

Side Coach: When the players start a new scene with the line that ended the previous scene, make sure they are aware that it is a brand-new scene and not a continuation of the last one. Every scene should be new and unrelated. The main difference between this game and Starting Line / Finish Line is that a line will begin and end two different scenes.

Section 5
CHARACTER DEVELOPMENT

The previous sets of exercises have been designed to help the actors take risks, make honest responses, and learn to make use of some of the natural tools at their disposal. In a way, they all lead to this last chapter.

These next games will explore ways to add layers to an actor's characters, hopefully making them something other than just the actor. By making choices with voice, mannerisms, gestures, physical traits, internal attributes, and emotions, they can develop their characters into individuals with a sense of their own person.

Makes Me Mad

Number of Players: Any number

Objective: To help actors raise their energy levels and experiment with emotional response

Description: The director will choose some frustrating topics and assign them to a series of players, one after another. The player will have 30 seconds to one minute, at the director's discretion, to commit to ranting and raving and getting this frustration off his or her chest. The rest of the audience is encouraged to get involved and support the emotional expression of the player.

Example:

DIRECTOR: OK, the first Makes Me Mad topic is "pushy sales people." Janet, you go first.

JANET *(storming onto the stage):* You know what really makes me mad?

AUDIENCE *(ad-lib):* No, what? What? Tell us.

JANET: Pushy sales people.

AUDIENCE *(joining in):* Yeah. Boo. Ow, I hate them.

JANET: They just won't leave you alone. You want to buy a blouse, and they want to sell you a dress . . .

(And so on.)

Side Coach: Encourage the audience to get involved and help all players commit to the feelings they have with their own frustrating topic. Make sure the players stay with it for the whole time period you've assigned them. Then when they are finished, they can end with, "That really makes me mad," and the audience can give them a round of applause. It is important that the players understand that it is not volume that's crucial, rather their commitment to the emotion and attitude of the exercise.

Changing Emotions

Number of Players: One at a time

Objective: To help an actor link the expression of emotion with physical expression. Movement is directly affected by motivation.

Description: Director can ask many players to think through this exercise on their own, perhaps in different parts of the room, before anyone volunteers to perform in front of the group. The player must complete a physical activity that for some reason must be undone using the same objects but with a different inner emotion. The same activities can be carried out in reverse with different feelings for the objects.

Example: A young man is setting a dinner table for two—setting the plates and silverware and taking things out of the refrigerator. All the while we see the joy he expresses as he dances around the table, perhaps kissing the condiments in imagined anticipation of his loved one's arrival. He gets a call on the phone canceling the date and, in obvious disappointment, has to put the plates and the things back. He ends up by tossing the soup angrily down the garbage disposal.

Side Coach: Don't push the players to perform this in front of others if they feel uncomfortable, but do encourage them to work through it and connect movement with honest emotion. Discuss how a character's motivation will often change his or her movement.

Quirks and Ticks

Number of Players: Three

Objective: To encourage actors to develop and remember traits that can be used to create interesting and believable characters. To listen and respond.

Description: Three players are chosen. One player is asked to temporarily exit the room. The audience suggests four quirks or ticks that many people exhibit. The director can assign the two remaining players a Who, What, and Where for the scene. The third player is asked back into the room. The director instructs PLAYERS 1 and 2 to begin a scene where they are discussing PLAYER 3, among other things. In the course of the scene, they need to discreetly discuss the ticks and quirks of the character played by PLAYER 3. PLAYER 3 is to overhear their discussion and enter the scene upon believing that he or she knows what four ticks to exhibit. Play proceeds until PLAYERS 1 and 2 are sure PLAYER 3 has displayed and incorporated the four different quirks or ticks. They then can conclude the scene.

Examples: The ticks and quirks could include things like belching, whistling, singing TV themes, always quoting *Readers Digest,* picking one's nose, and so on. The ticks can be physical or verbal.

Side Coach: The two players onstage must carry on a scene and label the person that is offstage with the ticks suggested by the audience. Each actor should give two quirks or ticks. Writing the suggestions down out of view of PLAYER 3 might be helpful.

Mystery Box

Number of Players: Two or more

Objective: To help an actor quickly establish a character choice

Description: The director puts together (perhaps raiding the costume closet) a box full of random props and costume pieces. The collection could include hats, dresses, jackets, scarves, gloves, eye glasses, pipes, canes, blankets, neckties, umbrellas, shawls, or anything that would readily suggest a character. The players in the scene are chosen. They make a certain number of random drawings from the box and use these for the basis of their characters. The audience then decides the rest of the improv groundwork—the Who, What, and Where of the scene. The players begin the scene.

Side Coach: Encourage the players to make quick choices and stick to them in the scene. Often times, the costume can give an actor numerous ideas and sudden inspirations for characters.

Attitudes and Occupations

Number of Players: Any number

Objective: To help actors think of ways to identify and communicate character traits

Description: Players sit in a circle. Each player will get up and perform an activity that clearly defines an occupation. The director should instruct the players to think in terms of a character who has a name, an age, and an attitude toward life, and all those characteristics should be played physically. As each player acts out these character aspects, the other players should throw out descriptive words. The other players can say out loud what they perceive about the character that is being presented. The director can have each of the players present a character for the audience.

Example:

Possible Occupations

1. Carpenter
2. Doctor
3. Teacher
4. President
5. Car mechanic
6. Lawyer

Different Attitudes

1. Life owes me.
2. Everything's cool.
3. I hate this.
4. I'm lonely.
5. I never get what I want.

Side Coach: Discuss some of the choices made by the players. Can they be used in developing a believable character for stage? Encourage the actors to be specific in their choices and keep them clear.

Irritations

Number of Players: Two at a time

Objective: To help actors recognize realistic character traits—overcoming obstacles

Description: The director chooses two players and gives them a Who, What, and Where. One player needs to be telling the other player something very important—regular interaction between the two characters ensues. PLAYER 1 is also assigned a single physical irritation that he or she must deal with throughout the scene. The information being revealed is far too important to stop, so PLAYER 1 must deal with the irritation, but it still affects his or her actions. When the director concludes the exercise, he or she can switch focus to the other player and start again.

Example: PLAYER 1 needs to tell his brother about this wonderful woman he met. He thinks he's in love. However, in the midst of this important discussion, he can't get rid of this piece of corn between his teeth or this annoying fly buzzing around his head or this nagging headache or this tight underwear or this tight collar, or there's a sudden rainstorm, and so on.

Side Coach: Help encourage the players to stay on task. Keep focused on relating the story, but be constantly aware of the annoyance.

"Make the irritation affect the way you tell your story."

Changes

Number of Players: Four

Objective: To challenge the actors to think about several things at once and make quick, creative decisions as is often the demand in live performance

Description: The director sets up a typical foundation for improvisation—the Who, What, and Where—for four players. The players are then told that each can improvise only two lines in the course of the whole scene. The scene will be short, but that's good. The best choice would be for the players to refrain from saying their second line until the others have all said their first line. After finishing the two-line interaction between all of the players, have them repeat the scene exactly the same way, with the same movements and the same lines. If the players make mistakes, just have them start again and keep working it until they can duplicate the short scene exactly the same way more than once. Once this is accomplished, the director can now start making changes. The lines stay the same, but the director can layer on a different attitude or focus or emotion to the scene. The challenge for the players is to maintain the content of the scene but think about and apply the differing parameters to it.

Example: Some of the different elements that the director can layer on are:

Emotions

1. Fear
2. Paranoia
3. Anger
4. Romance
5. Ecstasy
6. Jealousy

Physical Qualities

1. Hyperactive
2. Underwater
3. On the moon
4. As if in an earthquake
5. Death

Theatre Styles

1. Like Shakespeare
2. Musical comedy
3. Children's theatre
4. Gilbert and Sullivan
5. Grand Opera

Film Styles

1. Arnold Schwarzenegger movie
2. A Woody Allen movie
3. Film noir
4. Alfred Hitchcock
5. Horror film
6. Comedy
7. A Quentin Tarantino movie

Television

1. MTV
2. Soap opera
3. Sitcom
4. Cartoon

Or ask for suggestions from the rest of the audience.

Side Coach: Try not to let the players feel overwhelmed by the various challenges you throw at them. Help them see it as a fun experience that has no win or lose result. It's just a way of stretching past that with which they may be comfortable. It can be surprisingly rewarding to see what everyone comes up with.

Animal Party

Number of Players: Four to six

Objective: To explore variations in character characteristics and qualities

Description: The players should be placed randomly about the playing area. The audience will assign each of them an animal. Once they have each been given an animal, the director will instruct each player to begin imitating that animal, even to the point of crawling on hands and knees. After determining that each of the players has found some key characteristic of the assigned animal, the director can ask the players to begin making the animal more human. The goal is to eventually regain humanity while retaining some of the animal's characteristics. The director, satisfied with the players' choices, can then instruct them to interact as if they were at an office party or social event. The players should then let the animal characteristics influence their interaction and behavior toward each other.

Side Coach: "How will being a monkey and a lion affect your behavior with each other?"

Think of other places the animal/humans could meet:

1. An office
2. The theatre
3. School office
4. Bank
5. Library
6. An antique shop

Emotional Living Room

Number of Players: Two

Objective: To help actors explore emotional response along with thinking about multiple responsibilities onstage. A great exercise to help actors forget about their bodies and use their acting space.

Description: Divide the playing area into three sections. Each area will represent a different part of an efficiency apartment: for example, area one—the kitchen; area two—the living room with couch; area three—the entry way with a wall phone. Next, assign each area an emotional response: for example, area one—anger; area two—paranoia; area three—giddiness. Next, the director can choose two players and give them a relationship and a conflict to deal with. The players then need to enter the playing area using the three areas as they would in normal life, but also justifying the particular emotional response that is assigned to each area. The players should use the conflict they are struggling with to help move them through the apartment. Transitions from one part of the apartment to another and, therefore, one emotion to another should always be justified. The players can be together in a given area or separate but must be in all three areas at some point in the exercise.

Example: Players are husband and wife. The conflict is centered on the fact that he has been transferred to Alaska and she hates the cold. Area one is assigned passion; area two assigned love; area three assigned anger.

(They enter the scene.)

WOMAN *(moves to area two couch):* Sit here with me, honey. Let's snuggle.

MAN *(moves to area two couch):* I love you. What a meal, huh?

WOMAN: Uh-huh, sweety.

MAN *(standing and moving to area one):* Boy, I feel great, and I've got great news.

WOMAN *(gushy):* What is it, snuggle wuggums?

MAN: I got a great promotion and a transfer today.

WOMAN *(surprised):* What? *(Stands and moves to area three—suddenly angry)* You got a what?

Side Coach: Encourage the players to always be aware of where they are on the playing area and justify and exhibit the proper emotion.

"You're in anger now."

"Remember, if you move to her, you need to transition into passion."

Section 6
BONUS VOCAL WARM-UPS

As a special but short bonus, we are including a few vocal exercises too. To be great onstage, you have to be heard and understood. These few quick exercises can help.

1. Choose a four-line nursery rhyme such as "Mary Had a Little Lamb" or "Twinkle, Twinkle, Little Star." Using a controlled deep breath, practice saying the complete four lines from memory until you can say them slowly two times in one breath. Control the output of air so that it is depleted as the second jingle ends.

2. Practice to say all 11 of the following tongue twisters. Concentrate on keeping each word clean and clearly understandable. A well-enunciated speech can be understood at a great distance without yelling. (A friend at a Los Angeles voice-over class had to do all 11 lines in 30 seconds for his graduation. Can you?)

   a. Amos Ames, the amiable aeronaut, aided in an aerial enterprise at the age of 88.

   b. Some shun sunshine. Do you shun sunshine?

   c. Fine white wine vinegar with veal.

   d. Bring a bit of buttered brown bran bread.

   e. Geese cackle, cattle low, crows caw, cocks crow.

   f. Eight gray geese in a green field grazing.

   g. Six thick thistle sticks.

   h. Lucy likes light literature.

   i. A big black bug bit a big black bear.

   j. Peter Prangle, the prickly prangly pear picker, picked three pecks of prickly prangly pears from the prickly prangly pear trees on the pleasant prairies.

   k. Theopholus Thistle, the successful thistle sifter, in sifting a sieveful of unsifted thistles, thrust 3,000 thistles through the thick of his thumb. Now if Theopholus Thistle, the successful thistle sifter, in sifting a sieveful of unsifted thistles, thrust 3,000 thistles through the thick of his thumb, see that thou in sifting a sieveful of unsifted thistles thrust not 3,000 thistles through the thick of thy thumb. Success to the successful thistle sifter.

3. Choose a short (two- to four-minute) scene with two characters speaking to each other. Read the scene aloud using separate, relaxed character voices and incorporating dramatic inflections.

4. A knowledgeable vocal coach once told me that the best objective of any vocal warm-up is to accomplish two things:

   a. Get air moving away from your body.

   b. Set your sound in a forward placement.

Both of these activities help slowly warm the voice so that you won't strain it in normal stage use. A vocal exercise used by most singing coaches is to start in the midrange of your voice and move down the musical scale by half notes singing the word "nah." They usually use a five-step pattern down the scale, then raise or lower the next pattern by a half step.

When you use a musical vocal warm-up, perhaps combined with a spoken warm-up as listed above, you should always give yourself about 10 minutes of unpushed, relaxed vocal activity to properly loosen and warm up your vocal equipment. A warmed-up voice is a happy voice, and you won't sound like Gravel Gertie to boot.

DEFINITION OF TERMS

Audience: Observers. Those outside the actual physical participation of the games, such as remaining classmates, other acting team, or cast members.

Director: See Side Coach.

Exercise: Theatre games.

Improvisation: Spontaneous actions and choices made by actors that affect characters, objects, and a theatrical environment.

Gibberish: Meaningless sound representing recognizable words.

Objective: Goal; something worked toward.

Player: An actor—whether in a class, drama ministry, or workshop; one who participates in creating theatrical reality.

Playing Area: Designated area for the use of playing theatre games.

Scene: What evolves from playing out roles in interaction of stage characters.

Side Coach: A teacher or director who assists fellow players in exploring the creation of and adjustments in a given space.

Tools: Talents and abilities each actor possesses.

Verbalization: Revealing the structure of a scene by using words.

What: Activities or desired objectives (usually leading to a conflict) for actors as it relates to a scene or exercise.

Where: Imaginary environment; location for any given scene or exercise to occur.

Who: The relationship between the actors in a given scene or exercise.

ALPHABETICAL INDEX OF GAMES